Eggs in the Lake

BOA EDITIONS
NEW POETS OF AMERICA SERIES

Eggs in the Lake

poems by Daniela Gioseffi

foreword by John Logan

BOA EDITIONS • BROCKPORT, NEW YORK • 1979

Completion of this book was made possible by a grant award in poetry from The Creative Artists Public Service Program funded by The New York State Council on the Arts and the National Endowment for the Arts. I am grateful for the encouragement and financial assistance from CAPS.   — Daniela Gioseffi

The Publication of *Eggs in The Lake* was made possible with the assistance of a grant from the National Endowment for the Arts in Washington, D.C., a Federal agency.

Grateful acknowledgment is made to the editors of the following journals in which these poems first appeared: *Ambit* (Britain), *Antaeus, Assembling, Black Box, Bones, Chelsea, Choice, Cloud Marauder, The California Review, Dialog* (Canada), *Equal Time, Goliards, Hanging Loose, Italian-Americana, Migration, Modern Poetry Studies, Ms., The Nation, New Letters, The New York Quarterly, The Paris Review, Poet Lore, Poetry Now, Penumbra, Quadrant* (Australia), *Some, Sunbury, Sundial, Survivor's Manual, The Seminary Review of Friends School, Telephone, Toothpaste* and *The World.*

Grateful acknowledgment is also made to the editors and publishers of anthologies in which some of these poems, or earlier versions of them, were first published: "Quantum Poem" in *Contemporaries,* Jean Malley and Hale Tokay, Eds., The Viking Press, New York, 1972; "The Vases of Wombs," "Wearing Breasts," "Peace Prospect," "Woman with Tongue in Cheek" in *Rising Tides: 20th Century American Women Poets,* Laura Chester and Sharon Barba, Eds., Pocket Books, A Division of Simon & Schuster, New York, 1973; "Some Slippery Afternoon," "Vacancy," "Paradise Is Not a Place" in *We Become New: Poems by Contemporary American Women,* Lucille Iverson and Kathryn Ruby, Eds., Bantam Books, New York, 1975; "Some Slippery Afternoon," "Through the Eye of the Needle," "Eggs" in *The Ardis Anthology of New American Poetry,* David Rigsbee and Ellendea Proffer, Eds., The Ardis Press, Ann Arbor, Michigan, 1977.

"The Vases of Wombs," "Peace Prospect" and "Eggs" were recorded by the author on *Black Box 4* (A Cassette Magazine), Washington, D.C., 1974.

"Belly Dancer" and "The Earth Is Feminine In Most Languages" appeared in *The Great American Belly Dance,* a novel by Daniela Gioseffi, Doubleday & Co., Inc., New York, 1977, and in The New English Library edition of that novel, London, England, 1978.

Printed at the Visual Studies Workshop.
Cover Photo by DiGesare
Typeset by Advertising and Marketing Graphics.
Binding by Gene Eckert, Inc.

Distributed by the Book Bus, Visual Studies Workshop
31 Prince Street, Rochester, New York, 14607

ISBN 0-918526-13-2 Cloth
      0-918526-14-0 Paper

First Edition: January, 1979

For Josephine and Daniel Gioseffi, for the good friends who have encouraged me during the past ten years in which these poems were written, and for my daughter, Thea.

contents

foreword

I find Daniela Gioseffi's poems imaginatively rich, start-
ling, intelligent (with a wide range of reading behind them)
and eloquent in a manner relevant to one of the most pro-
found issues of our time: the relationship of the masculine
and the feminine principles inside the self and society. A
feminist writer who celebrates what it is to be a woman,
Ms. Gioseffi is also genuinely a poet whose work comes
from the part of the personality that gives, shares and
creates bonds rather than from the part that is divisive
and militant. Fortunately, there is little politics here —
something ill-suited to poetry. And there are very few
feminist writers of which this can be said.

Ms. Gioseffi is inventive, usually in a surreal mode, and she
shares with the lyric poet generally that loneliness which
comes from the struggle with the self. "In My Craft or
Sullen Art" is the title of a poem by Dylan Thomas, and
we remember that the word "sullen" comes from the Latin
"solus" which means "alone." Yet when the poetic *gift of
sharing* is present, by which I mean making public in a
beautiful fashion, as it is in Ms. Gioseffi's work, then that
loneliness — which is itself part of the human condition —
becomes altered ironically and one is not alone in the same

way as before the experience of art. Rather, one is brought, through the poetry, what Dylan Thomas called "a temporary peace". This "peace" I see as the natural equivalent to grace.

Ms. Gioseffi brings us such moments again and again. "I am a lost and primitive priestess/" she writes, "wandering in a walled city of the wrong century." Still, "I would have been what you were searching for/ . . . if you could decide/what sleeper you resemble and which of your dreams/struggles behind your eyelids."

There is also a special kind of loneliness Ms. Gioseffi writes about in a poem titled "The Loneliness of the Pregnant Woman":

> She dreams
> trees push limbs up
> through her belly; her body
> is an oven breaking bread, a moon
> presses from between her lips,
> floats, a loaf of sun in winter light.

I want to comment on two further aspects of this passage. One is the image of the tree — Ms. Gioseffi has struck an archetypal note here, for the changing of the woman into a tree (cf. also her poem "My Venus Flytrap is Dying") occurs again and again in the history of literature, from Ovid's story of Daphne through Dante to modern poems of Ezra Pound, Hart Crane, and James Wright. (The title poem of Wright's most recent book, "To a Blossoming Pear Tree," is a beautiful piece about the transformation of a woman into a tree.) Norman O. Brown has an essay in which he sees the metamorphosis of Daphne as being at the very heart of poetry itself. "Undulate the branches of your arms/in the wind, goddess of trees," Ms. Gioseffi writes in another poem.

The other motif in this poem I want to note is the andro-
gynous one which is introduced by the juxtaposition of the
feminine moon with the masculine sun. I believe that one
of the deepest motives for writing is man's attempt to feel
his way into the world of woman and woman's attempt to
feel her way into the world of man. This is not opposed to
the search for self-identity on the part of man or woman
poet for each finds the other at the heart of self. In another
poem of Ms. Gioseffi's she uses an epigraph from Rimbaud
which combines the theme of self-identity and androgyny:
"The poets of the future will come when the infinite servi-
tude of woman will be broken, when she will live for her-
self and by herself . . . she will also be poet! Woman will
find the unknown! . . . The two sexes will then make
one . . . the great Androgyne will be created, humanity will
be woman and man, love and thought, tenderness and
strength, grace and energy."

Ms. Gioseffi's "The Sea Hag in the Cave of Sleep" is one
of the most ambitious androgynous poems of our time.
Here the lines occur, "He swims into me in clouds of
semen," and "Sea and shore mix in one giant sex." The
poem ends with the astonishing image of the female assum-
ing the penis at the moment of giving birth: "I come out
from between my own legs into this world."

As in all lyric poetry there is a strong search for identity
by the speaker in these poems: "I can be anything I will
myself to be. I spend all my time . . . willing to be/what
always/I am about to become." Again, "a vast lonely con-
science strains to give itself a name." Here is a quotation
from her work which reflects the eternal yearning of the
poet for an audience who will help him assert his identity:
"I wake . . . /and think there must be someone there . . .;
who listens to me here in the dark."

Yet the poems present a very strong self-identity of the speaker as woman. In "Caves" Ms. Gioseffi writes: "At the hour of sleep a woman enters her own body/through mouths hidden beneath the skirt of night." Though there is compassion for the hardships of a woman's life, as in the elegiac words for her grandmother ("She died, her body wearied/from giving and giving and giving/food and birth.") still the overall tone of the book is the celebration of the status of woman — particularly in the essential creativity of the maternal impulse.

The poem "Caves," from which I quoted, is taken from a section of the book entitled "The Vases of Wombs" — a phrase in which Ms. Gioseffi reveals her unusual intelligence, for it is taken from her long and deep research into the historical and psychological development of the woman (in this case she is echoing Eric Neumann's monumental *The Great Mother*, which sees vases since ancient times as ikons so to speak of the woman's womb).

One of Ms. Gioseffi's poems, "The Belly Dancer," reminds us how far her researches have taken her: from her reading she discovered that what has come to be called "the belly dance" was in reality a *birth* dance given by women to assist at and celebrate the births of children. The dance originally had nothing to do with the market place and the entertainment of men. She has acted on her own research and learned the art of the "birth dance", frequently supplementing her programs with lectures on the dance and readings from her poems. She has written and published a novel called *The Great American Belly Dance* (Doubleday 1977; Dell 1978).

On this aspect of Ms. Gioseffi's work one cannot do better than to look at an article on her poems by Harold Schechter entitled "The Return of Demeter: The Poetry of Daniela Gioseffi" (*Psychocultural Review* Vol. I, pp. 452-

457). Schechter in a Jungian analysis reminds us that behind androgyny lies sysygy, the union and vital exchange from the heart of the feminine to the heart of the masculine and vice versa, and he also reminds us that in promoting the matriarchal over the patriarchal — in particular that aspect of the former which is benevolently maternal (creative) as opposed to the vengeful, terrible "tooth" mother (cf. Robert Bly's poem "The Teeth Mother Naked at Last") one is promoting a healthier, richer society — a society of hope — the newer, higher order which Ms. Gioseffi presents in her poem "Peace Prospect": "A better race will come./I feel/bright animals waiting/for the right genetic moment."

Still it is not in such partly didactic poems as "Peace Prospect" that I feel Ms. Gioseffi's strength so much as in those which dramatize a genuine erotic moment ("We might touch ourselves into peace") or show a deep rapport with other created things — rapport with sun, sea and salt in "Beyond the East Gate," with plants in "Talking to My Philodendron," or with ancient creatures of the deep as in "Wearing Breasts" and in "For Prince Myshkin."

Because so much of Ms. Gioseffi's work touches the common, deep experiences of mankind (what Jung would call archetypes of the collective unconscious) I believe Jung should have the last word here in our approach to her poetry. "Whenever the collective unconscious becomes a living experience and is brought to bear upon the conscious outlook of an age, this event is a creative act which is of importance to everyone." Need I add this means you and me.

John Logan

John Logan
Mayday, 1978

13

I. Beyond the East gate

Reality invents me,
I am its legend!
                    — Jorge Guillen

I saw them despoil themselves, sobbing and
singing, for a hen's egg . . .
                    — Frederico Garcia Lorca

BEYOND THE EAST GATE

I listen to the voice of the cricket,
loud in the quiet night,
warning me
not to mistake a hill for a mountain.
I need to be alone,
in a private house with doors that open only outward,
safe from strangers who smell of death,
where I can draft a universe under my eyelids
and let nothing invade it.

I want to sing a fugue
sounding like the genius of flowers
talking to leaves on their stems,
to have more concrete meaning
than even the dance of a child in my uterus.
I'm a lost and primitive priestess
wandering in a walled city of the wrong century.
I need to spend thirty years in the desert
before I will understand the sun,
thirty years at sea
to gather the blessing of salt and water.

In the back room of my skull
a secret dice game determines
the rites of my hands
before they touch flesh again.
I want to reach a peace I've never known,
to be an old woman who is very young,
a child who is a sage
come down from the mountain.

TALKING TO MY PHILODENDRON

Green passion on the horizon of my waking,
Leaves, whose green yawn matches mine with
        morning,
whose breath is always sweet,
pristine peace and super-human silence,
whose beauty is never coveted by men nor envied
by women, whose constancy depends on waters
of my memory, hear me; feel me loving you,
playing Mozart concertos for you.

I test your soil for moisture, feel
of you adoringly,
sense you answer me,
in the dark tube of your stem,
speak to me in the veins of your heart.
Lift the fingery hands on the wrists of your stems
and wave at me;
tell me you hear me, feel
dreams flow through me into yours,
my senses, your perception through long nights;
seep through me as water in your cells.

Leaves, understand the peace
I sigh into you. Let me know I long
to be with you, my body
melting to earth caressed by roots,
gentle open palms against my red eyes,
green hands of the Goddess
on the heart of my vegetal sleep,
on the breast, leaves, of my animal dreams.

WEARING BREASTS

I sit back in the city
and admire the octopus,
wise old mollusk.

I myself am an ancient fish
wearing new plastic shoes.
My lungs have been through many changes —
breathing water, then ooze, then air.
A tree-climbing fish evolved me,
giving me delicate names:
Ivy, Heather, Rose, Lily,
and a cave of sleep within my body,
a child's room
with a closed flower to guard the entrance.

Out of the estuaries
where rivers come to the sea,
I am born of my mother's waters
and can't find my paternal parent
or give wifely comfort
among creatures that stare from green mud.

FOR PRINCE MYSHKIN

When I ride the adventures of my legs through your
    heart,
or complain of bathroom spiders crawling up my ankles
as I wash blood from my thighs,
when I call to you from nightmares,
want you to be a wave pulling me out to sea,
or beg you to assure my voice is etched on glass
    eardrums,
when I go leaving behind a sink full of winter,
I need to swallow my agony,
be told, "You are, you are a child again!"

I poke at your petals like a child,
twisting your stem until you break
and your pollen falls around you.
I gather and examine it in trembling hands.
I know that you are pure, the ideal idiot,
but I am trying to understand you
through a periscope.
I'm a lonely submarine of ripe flesh
swimming with the blind,
crusted creatures of the deep.

EGGS

—for Francis Ponge

Eggs that come from chickens,
squeezing oblong from their feathered bottoms.
Tapered ovals opaque with white
filled with albumen. Delicate thickness!
I've eaten them raw, sucking them from a pin-hole
carefully made in the shell.
I've pressed my lips to the hole and sucked
until the white carried the yolk out in one mass onto
    my tongue.
I've beaten them and butter-fried them into spongy
    yellow chunks.
I've left their sunny sides up
until the whites were glazed like plastic,
and then pricked the orange yolk with the sharp
    point of a fork
and watched it slowly spread and ooze over the plate.
Then, I've sopped it up with toast
until the toast was soggy and limp
and dripped when lifted to the mouth.
I've boiled them and listened
to the click of shells
as they wobbled in the bubbling water.
Small sounds of thunder; shell against metal.
I've cracked them and peeled them,
pulling the residue of skin-like membrane from them,
then sliced or bit into their shine of rubbery white
with its yellow paste center.
I've lathered them into my hair with shampoo,
mixed them with cheeses and mushrooms and onions.

Today I've brought one hundred dozen of them —
farm-fresh, Grade A, large white eggs in
spongy, grey, cardboard cartons.
I've arranged them around

the bathroom, their cartons opened, exposing
rows of gleaming white lumps.
One thousand two hundred of them!
Delicate shells threaten to burst and spray yolk over
    tile.
I choose the first, tap it lightly on the porcelain tub.
A thin line shatters the cool shell.
I violate the crack, thumb-nail first, slowly
separate the shell, tearing
the inside membrane with a small sound of skin, and
plop it into the tub.
Its nucleus of yellow pops on the hard surface below.
Slowly, from the ragged half-shell
a clear string of mucus, a long thin globule, follows
after it. I take the next
and the next, crack
each on the tub edge, plop
it to the hard surface, see
the yellow yolks break, ooze, and splatter.
I keep on with my work
till the tub fills enough for me to watch
the yolks bounce into the thick
liquid, sink a little, then buoy to the surface.
When I drop, at last, the-one-thousand-two-hundreth,
the tub is full; the mucoid surface
is cobbled with yolks. Slowly,
I put one bare leg into the tub, letting the viscous
mass climb up my body as I slide
down in up to my chin. I lie
perfectly still, listening
to the silent squish of the mass that surrounds me.
I smear the fluid into my hair and over my skin,
I move and thrash my limbs about
until the mixture of yolk and white
is thoroughly blended.

AT THE BANK OF A LAKE

Black sedans the mayor ordered
from the city
invade rows of trees,
arrive at the bank of a lake
where water polishes stones.

Wheels hum, engines purr,
cool water laps and ripples.
Fish leap,
birds dive
with watery sounds
into the lake.

Keys turn; engines die.
The sun sinks into the horizon,
gleams in the fenders of each sleek sedan.
Behind sheer glass windows
old men's faces stare, somber with grey
beards, long noses, tight mouths.

Each eye
of each old man's face
reflects
the pin-point image
of a naked moonlit woman
asleep beside a lake.

SUSANNAH TO THE ELDER

Eyes that pierced my nakedness,
invading the privacy of my bath,
did not harm me.
They were as innocent as nipples
chilled erect by cold water.

When I see your naked body,
your limp genitals lying in your lap,
even though I am far younger,
I feel a mother to you,
what the earth is to a tree.

Don't be afraid.
Your aging body has it's own beauty
and I would give my youth to you
if my innocence did not frighten you,
or if you would take my kisses like grapes
to quench your thirst.

But your eyes are frightened,
staring at the purple fruit,
bubbled with the cool sweat of washing,
cupped in the hands I hold out to you.

You see a tiny fetus,
glistening red,
curled inside of each transparent grape skin.
You cringe, cover yourself with guilt,
as the white teeth in my small red mouth
crush the juice from one.

THE LILY PAD

Morning:

She pulls a French horn from the bodice of her dress,
tries to play it.
No sound comes out.
She begins to weep
but the cries she makes
sound like a horn played
far off in the distance.

Noon:

She puts the French horn back into the bodice of her
    dress,
runs to the river,
leaps in,
the weight of the horn
carries her to the bottom.
The same water fills her ears
that flows through the horn.
She hears its sound
sighing in her head.

Night:

She swims to the surface dragging the French horn
    with her.
Her hair has turned white.
She drowns with the horn clutched to her shrivelling
    lips.
Her white hair floats out all around her:
Now she is a lily pad
with a frog
singing on her breast.

II. Vacancy

Psychology which explains everything explains
nothing,
and we are still in doubt.
— Marianne Moore

The immediate beauty of a rag in the wind . . .
The immense stone statue of a grain of sea salt
The joy of every day and the uncertainty of dying
   and the iron of love in the wound of a smile . . .
— Jacques Prevert

SOME SLIPPERY AFTERNOON

A silver watch you've worn for years
is suddenly gone
leaving a pale white stripe
blazing on your wrist.

A calendar marked with all
the appointments you meant to keep
disappears
leaving a faded spot on the wall
where it hung.
You search the house, yard, trash cans
for weeks
but never find it.

One night the glass in your windows
vanishes
leaving you sitting in a gust of wind.

You think how a leg is suddenly lost
beneath a subway train
or a taxi wheel
some slippery afternoon.

The child you've raised for years,
combing each lock,
tailoring each smile, each tear,
each valuable thought,
suddenly changes to a harlequin,
joins the circus passing in the street,
never to be seen again.

One morning you wash your face,
look into the mirror,
find the water has eroded your features,
worn them smooth as a rock in a brook.
A blank oval peers back at you
too mouthless to cry out.

THE ORIGINS OF MILK

Mushrooms grow in my thighs
to spite the frenzy I've offered as love.
Faces explode my albums
with sighs that shatter gravestones.
Torn up for confetti, I'm showered
on the celebration winding in the streets below.
Another man is elected to rule the flow of milk.
I look for my mother copulating among sheep
in a dream field. A haze floats in over my head,
a long cold shore of sand.
I ask a genie waiting to be born
in blue smoke from my navel if
she has heard my magic words and knows
I, too, wish to see beyond the lamp.

All the telephone booths are out of order
in the soup of the city. Strange voices,
shells from unknown seas sound in my ears.
Stray dogs wander in gutters, nipping
at my toes. Abandoned children sit on curbs.
Panhandlers replace clowns on every corner.
They do not smile or dance, but simply ask
for money to be dropped in empty cups.
I ponder coins, weather maps, rubber stamps,
     newsprint,
white bread, false hair, plutonium.
Stranded in a society of abstracted men,
I am made of primal customs practiced in varied
     tongues.
I gather water, try to chat with you amidst flower-
     boxes.
Fumes clog my throat; machines follow me down the
     street,

grinding gears against flesh. Grey dials turn. I try
to call you whom I met by the accuracy of chance.
The telephone receiver is gone.
It's stuck to my mouth. My eyes
are dimes caught in my hair.

Blood I left on your sheets
came from moons of change hidden in my belly.
When we part, are you still there, are we
lovers as we were?
Curdling time gives us up to decisions.
Kettles whistle for morning coffee
and we mourn our dreams. I want
to bottle wind, drink it for cola. Instead,
I lose you among strange hands, open mouths,
wiggling buttocks, umbrellas.
I would have been what you were searching for
with sheer will, if you could decide
what sleeper you resemble and which of your dreams
struggles behind your eyelids.

I hardly bear the hollow music of a tubular life.
Birds in my inner ear batter wings to get out.
I have no names to call them to open windows.
The artful lover lacks artless feeling.
I knew when you touched me where your thoughts
        were.
I can't be fooled into orgasm, but I can pretend.
Into my chest, I follow birds, trying to sing
proper notes to the moon, mirroring the sun,
to the darkness in me, nothing without your light.
Perhaps the finest language is silence in its glory.
I long to be an apple tree standing in your garden.

QUANTUM POEM

I feel like a gingerbread man

        running from my destiny

meeting a hungry fox

        by the boiling sea

an oyster

        gone walking with a walrus

in either instance

        I keep disappearing

WOMAN WITH TONGUE SCULPTED IN CHEEK

There are no rules for sadness —
so much despair rising from the sink drains of evening.
The chairs are empty,
curtains full of wind,
the room silent as a lantern.
Who couldn't go on
spilling pages of wordy histories,
cracking thoughts as shells
from nutmeats of philosophies,
spinning threads from fish eyes.

I lift my breasts waiting for the ceiling
to sprout fingers.
Men do not let women live in their dreams
but dream of women in their lives
as if we could be as good as trees,
as calm as photosynthesis in all our fornication.

Guilty since Eve, I will not be responsible for
     temptation,
I pull the trap door shut, close my legs against
     eternity,
build a moat around my uterus,
use my ovaries for amulets,
cease rattling my bracelets,
cut off my nails
and close my lips tight against kisses, new mournings.

My hair was not my own idea;
it grew from his rays and he commanded
that I brush it till it shown as moonbeams
because he was the sun,
he was
everyone:
He was Dr. Kildare, Emmett Kelly, Christ;

Leonardo da Vinci, Albert Einstein, Louis Pasteur;
Charlemagne, Napoleon, Mozart, and Shakespeare;
Mailer, Ginsberg, Plato, and Buddha;
Lincoln, Rembrandt, Donato Gioseffi, and Richard
    Kearney.

Father, husband, whom I've worshipped all my years.
I've let you commit crimes in my name,
place me on a pedestal of halos,
hide my clitoris as my hips grew wider
and a child squeezed out of my heart,
grew big as a mountain,
swallowed me for dinner,
held me in a sucking grip until I crooned lullabies.

I've washed a thousand bathtubs
and watered a million geraniums
with the fallings of my dreams,
and the knight,
the Knight,
the night,
never comes riding never comes riding
never comes
riding
except to admonish me
for vanity he creates in me
or to drape a heavy blue robe around my shoulders
and rest his crucified body
in my soft and tired lap.

WARM KEYS

A lost love leaps from the fire of my brow.
I zipper him away.
I can't feed bears to angels.
Angels are not there.
Goodbye, my friends,
you've all turned into keyholes.
I'm no different than a camel or a tiger.
My ears bark at candles.
I try to burn all of Keats in the ashtrays.

Though I remember only the rhythm of his speech,
I carve a pear from memory
trying to bite his face into it.
Somewhere sand curves down into the pampering sea.
I think of all the rain
falling backwards toward the birth of money.

Chopin's Nocturnes bind my chest with wires.
A true lover that doesn't exist
tiptoes toward me, a thousand genitalia protrude
or gape from it.
It raises its head.
Its eyes are mirrors
arranged to reflect mirrors in me.
It opens its mouth,
revealing glass tongues coated with silver.

I feed it spittle from my mouth
and it sings an ancient lullaby
audible only to the trees.

VACANCY

Faceless, I chase you
frantically through the museum
begging you to paint eyes on my face.
You slip away
disgusted by my whining need of you.

I ask the guard who looks like my father
the way to the powder room.
He pulls out his shining tube,
smears a lipstick mouth on my blank face
and says: "Speak!"
I try, but my red mouth slips down my chin,
staining my collar.

I rush into the street.
The crowds stare in horror
at the naked oval of my head.
I attempt to unscrew it from my neck
and stuff it in the first litter basket I meet.

Waking far outside myself,
I find I lie beside you.
You do not stir in your sleep
or feel the darts, questions I fire
at your numbed head.

  "Am I all right this way, headless without a face?"
I say. "Shall I be plump or thin, intelligent, dumb,
bold, demure, famous, obscure, sister, wife, mother,
thief, giver, jealous, indifferent, poet, madman
or lover, or just work in the Five and Dime
and cook your supper?"

You tell me, father, husband,
I can be anything I will myself to be.
I spend all my time
willing,
willing to be
what always
I am about to become.

SEQUEL

Each day ends, a record left turning.
I lift the needle,
place it back in its cradle,
not to end sound, but
to end silence with silence.
When prayer-plants fold their leaves
together like hands at dusk,
a smiling corpse rules twilight,
smuggles the sun beneath his cloak.

At sunset, I talk to myself
as if to God,
hoping for an answer.
I watch bees swarm, and
view the city from rooftops,
see points of light, ideas set afire,
dot the skyline.
The copper sun dips into the harbor
to bathe itself,
then sinks beyond the curve.

In the middle of the night
I wake, listen to silence,
and think there must be someone there
waiting
who listens to me here in the dark
and thinks
there must be someone there
waiting in the silence.

III. The Vases of Wombs

"Physical or 'real' birth is really rebirth,
a repetition of an archetypal birth of the
cosmos from the cosmic egg."
— Norman O. Brown
Love's Body

"I understand the tree, it does not
reason . . . . Fawns you have had your
day: the poet now wants to talk to the
tree."
— Jules Renard

"The Woman-Soul leadeth us . . . on!"
— Johann von Goethe

THE LONELINESS OF THE PREGNANT WOMAN

A kick at her inner walls,
a thud rising in her throat,
half wakes her in the dark. Her hand
slides beneath cloth over smooth
stretched skin. Another kick, flesh
against flesh, tingles her palm.
She pushes back blankets,
feels a mound of earth
rising from her
womb. She dreams
trees push limbs up
through her belly; her body
is an oven baking bread, a moon
presses from between her lips,
floats, a loaf of sun in winter light.

In mourning, she buys red apples
in place of roses
for her mother's grave. She carries
them like eggs through marching throngs,
gliding carefully between man-
made objects, bringing apples to the cemetery.
Knives and guns sticking, poking out
from windows, doors, alleyways,
might burst
the delicate dirigible, her hope
singing earthy songs in her.

THE VASES OF WOMBS
—for The Venus of Willendorf

For a long time,
I've thought about this body of mine
with agony, with curiosity, and dreams
of caressing lovers and children.

I've thought about these arms
as if they belonged to an Etruscan priestess
raising them over her head to pray or protect hunters,
or were handles on the hips of an ancient Greek vase
pedestaled in the still light of a museum.
I've listened to the blood flowing through them
or crossed them over my breasts to imagine rest.
I've thought about these buttocks,
how they've held me to the earth while others fly
and inhabit the high shelves of libraries.
I've thought about these peering nipples,
feelers on a cat's face sensitive to night.

Men accept mead, soma, nectar from my hands,
blood from my womb, fish from my eyes,
crystals from my eardrums, food from my glands.
In return, they try to pierce the heart
that ticks between my thighs
pinning me to the bed like a butterfly.

These arms fly out of themselves to talk to you.
This head becomes small and sightless.
These breasts and buttocks swell
until they're all that's left of me, until
I'm melted into earth and planted as a garden.

CAVES

At the hour of sleep a woman enters her own body
through mouths hidden beneath the skirt of night.
Inside the darkness, moist and quiet,
she dreams of all the cavernous wombs of nature
hidden from the light:

Caves, temples for gods or monarchs' chambers,
chandeliered with stalactites formed drop by antique
    drop,
underground streams worn through limestone;
caves from which we first yawn awake
pressing out between lips, exits from, entrances to
    death,
arched by thighs like swords at a wedding;
caves haunted by sibyls, nymphs, cyclops;
deep hollows in the sides of sea cliffs
battered in by tides, blown open by eruptions
of hot lava; galleries, sink holes reaching
up to earth like open drains;
ears vibrating with music,
sighing with sea sounds of shells;
nostrils breathing rose, sage, sandalwood;
stomachs churning food to pulp, echoing with hunger;
mouths sucking, swallowing, biting kissing;
womanly caves to which men return again
and again to burrow back into earth,
to curl up in like bears, squirrels, bees, hibernating
through winter, safe with their acorns, honey, semen,
sleeping snugly in the belly of a tree,
waiting like eggs to begin.

THE SEA HAG IN THE CAVE OF SLEEP

"For all the bold and bad and bleary
they are blamed, the sea hags."
— James Joyce, *Finnegans Wake*

Words whirl her round in pools.
I cling by my teeth, grinding mountains.
She floats. I scream. She drops
through an eternity of light.
I float again. I fall
calling for animals to warm her,
pleading with trees to feed me.

Darkness fills her like a carbohydrate.
Ponds ooze; crickets drone in black space.
A snake slides over a rock;
a seed is dragged to another grave.
Human voices hum behind the stones;
a vast, lonely conscience
strains to give itself a name.

The cave of sleep opens as she spreads her legs.
The father enters the iridescent dark from which he
     came.
Blocks of ice fall from his aging flesh. She turns to him
to marry him and be his mother again. When she turns
     again
she is his son. The shine of his skin slides
down her throat. Seaweed glides through my limbs.
     Kisses.
Kisses. Land and water come together in the mud of
     our lips
crawling with tongues that give touch to words.
He swims into me in clouds of semen.
Babies cry in our mouths. We float from the warm well
in aboriginal kisses.

Lizards nestle in bushes
hurting and loving the leaves;
landbirds peck at tortoise shells.
She feels how wet the earth is,
nearly all water.
Since she first bled
there has been a passion finer
than lust, as if everything living is
moist with her.
She knows the language of leaves
as an animal blessed with it.

In the trees is a clue to everything
and a happy one, like the genesis
of estrogen. Ever since
the first woman bled, plants cry when
animals are murdered; hands think
as bees emoting sweet sweat;
apples are made for eating;
even mathematics is glandular;
an algebra of feelings.
Only wars are waged
in the guise of pure perception
as though flesh were an alloy of aluminum,
or an isolated element.

She takes off her dress;
she lifts off her breasts;
she has a talk with the sparrows
who inhabit my chest.
She is divided by contrary loves I have taken in.
When I open her legs a river of contradiction flows
    from me.
Her limbs are estuaries rippling toward my stomach.
She drowns inside myself
longing for a god to speak to her from her lover's
    tongue,

as they explode together in whirlpools of sperm and
    ova
spinning against the silence.

        When the baby came down out of her,
        it felt thick between my lips,
        squeezing out erect life. Its belly
        passed her clitoris as it came with
its cries of semen squirting from me. As its toes slid
    out
I was female again . . .

        A vast landscape accepts her with silence
        as if it were my private garden
        to gather stones from her sleep.
        The phantom of age descends the staircase!

        In the middle of the afternoon,
        when light is blinding,
        I am looking for a man with arms, tree-
            trunks,
        fingers, branches to turn her nipples
        green as spring buds. She waits outside my-
        self, for him to welcome her in.
        Or is it sleep, a peace deep as death,
        she wants from him?
        She puts on feathers like a bird
        or a chorus girl. He can't know which.

If he comes to her bed,
she will be an orgasm of birds singing in wet leaves.
The mouth of my dream will be open forever.
I'll burst with a child, time hurdled from her throat.
She will paint a song beneath my eyelids
to sing into his sighs:

        Down by the water
        silver-haired witches are dancing,

down by the water,
tossing their curls.
Their breasts are eyes
from which the sea rises.
In their mouths the sea cries.
They are kicking the sand
made from our bones.
Silver-haired witches
down by the water,
singing and dancing,
playing with bones.

We take for each other
the place of absent gods.
We bargain for the eyes of fish
to swim in an underground stream
longing for no death.

> These are our plum pits,
> petrified and strung
> These are our beetles gleaming in the coal.
> We have come shining in ice from the mud
> trailing seaweed in our wings of bone.

We read;
we write books;
from the deep spring of orgasm flowing in the flesh,
we erupt in cataleptic fits
as faith from the insane.
We will invent love until the sea closes in.

> The phantom of age ascends the staircase;
> a vast landscape accepts me with silence;
> I gather stones from her sleep.

She has knitted him a shawl
and come to the frayed ends of history.
His fingers are no longer primal myths kneading her.

Sea and shore mix in one giant sex.

In the index of my womb, I find her face . . .
She is no spider queen after all,
        She is a green beast with arms of sorrow . . .

Her whole body is a phallus . . .

        I come out from between my own legs
        into this world.

BELLY DANCER

An Etruscan priestess
through whom the earth speaks,
enters veiled; a mystery
moves toward the altar.
Unknown features, shadow of death, of brows,
of eyes, mouth, lips, teeth of the night,
jaw thrust forward like a pelvis,
navel hidden, mysterious circuit,
electrical wire of the first cries
thrust from the womb.
The silk covering hovers over her,
turns with a whirling gesture
round as the moon that glows in her belly.
Her navel winks in a quiver.
Amazing belly that stretches large enough
to let a life grow.
She glides, dips, shimmies,
thrusts one hip, then another.
The music breaks. Pain
fills the drum. She
falls to her knees, doubles
over, leans back on her heels
as her stomach flutters, rolls
with contractions, upward, down-
ward, sinks her head into the floor,
raises her pelvis, arching, widening.
Arms rise like serpents from a flesh basket,
beat, caress, nip, shimmer the air with rhythmic
pulse. At last
the bloody mystery emerges,
inch by inch the head presses
through the lost hymen.
Her pain works into a smile.
The decked and bejeweled mother
pushes out her ecstasy.

The formless fluid shot into her,
molded, fired in the secret oven,
emerges, a child crying: it lives!
Its voice rings in her finger cymbals.

She rests her body, slowly
rises from the earth.
Her breasts fill with milk.
She shakes them:
this is food, I am food.

Woman, whose nerve-filled clitoris
makes her shiver, ecstatic
mother, dance with a fury
around your circle of women.
Spin out the time locked in your own womb,
bloom from your uterus,
Lady of the Garden.
The moon pulls you,
crashes waves on the shore.
Undulate the branches of your arms
in the wind, Goddess of Trees,
of all living things.
Your flesh is not defiled by
men who can't contain your mystic
energy of woman. Belly
that invites life to sleep in you,
breasts of mortal ambrosia,
Amazon groin that lit the hearth,
altar, oven, womb, bread
table, Earth
Mother, pagan
witch of magic birth,
from whom all suck
leaves that flow through the body's blood,
cave of your sex, our home,
moon of earth, Great Mother.

THE PEACH THROUGH THE EYE OF THE NEEDLE

I.

The peach
is a belly dancer's fruit.
It, too,
possesses a navel
for seeing the world through the skin,
has rounded buttocks, good
to place against the hand
the way earth
reminds flesh of its being.

II.

Through the eye of the needle,
death is a country where people wonder
and worry what it is like
to live. The sullen
wish to live and live soon,
to be done with death
and the happy
want to stay dead forever
wondering
will it hurt to live
and is there death after death.

NIPPLED TREES OUTLAST AN AGE OF STEEL

Lawn mowers and can openers hammered into arks
as cradles for bread will float
because She made the tower lean
after you built it.

Blizzards, gale winds, tidal waves, floods, sleet,
hail, tornadoes, fish frozen in the lake of Her mouth!
And you thought to tame Her, to hold Niagara
by the waist. To keep Her from eating kings' eyes
you built pyramids against sand storms.
To span Her rivers, you threw legs of steel
over Her thighs, gathered her fury like roses,
scoffed at the vulturism of the sea, took
what you wanted from Her, and refused
to give back what you threw away. You dreamed
of keeping her, a wife in a pumpkin shell, but
no cage holds the sea. When you tied down Her hair
with steel cables, She sent up a hurricane, smashing
concrete. Her necessity is your peace, Her mystery,
your gospel. You shall climb mountains in search
of berries. You shall walk through the forests to suck
Her breasts, cling as children at her skirts.
For every leg of a bridge thrown over Her,
she changed the course of a river, and so
you shall build your houses where She chooses
in the midst of wild grasses.

THE EARTH IS FEMININE IN MOST LANGUAGES:
A PSALM
(From an Essential Libretto for a New Age Symphony)

— after a passage in the
Taittiriya Upanishad 2.2.

From food comes all, all that lives upon the Earth.
All is food, and to food it shall return.
Food is the only goddess among the living.

They are blessed with food who worship earth,
for the Earth is food and goddess among the living.
All are born of food
and by food they grow.

The Goddess is Earth and food her panacea.
All are born of her food
and to food they shall return.
All eat Her
and she eats all.

Food we are
and to food we shall return.
That is why She is called Sugar! Blossom! Honey!

The Great Mother gave milk in the beginning.
She arose as a dream from mud
but from Her comes food and from food: breath, spirit,
        truth,
worlds, and in works, immortality.

IV. Peace Prospect

"That unity of culture and nature, work
and love, morality and sexuality for which
mankind is forever longing . . . will
remain a dream as long as man does not
permit the satisfaction of the biological
demands of natural orgasmic sexual
gratification . . . Until then, the
extinguishing of life will prevail, be it
in compulsive social institutions or in
wars."
      —Wilhelm Reich
      The Discovery of the Orgone

"Of physiology from top to toe I sing,
Not physiognomy alone or brain alone is
   worthy of the Muse.
I say the Form complete is worthier far,
The Female equally with the Male I sing."
      —Walt Whitman
      "I Sing the Body Electric"

MAJOR SURGERY

My dreams rise, a twist of smoke.
Spirits hammer at my throat
or sleep like pig iron in my belly.

I resolve to leave this hospital renewed.
An antique bird
will fly on metal wings
changed to feathers.
What is made of wood in my life
remains fresh, unvarnished.

All stories close like cupboards,
cracked teacups line up on shelves.
I lick ether from my fingers,
roll my eyes back in my head.
There were houses,
many photographs in albums.

Ants crawl toward a hill
to be crushed
when the shoe descends into evening.

Cars buzz in the walls.

FALLING INTO SAND

Yearning rests in the sea:
a bottle floating messages
answers to the secret future.
We talk of the end
as the driest thing there is.
Forests burn into their clearings:
a sense of dread, flags
of an age of huge weapons,
poison gases, nitrates, analysis.
Angry factories send the day into smoke.
Minerals are asleep in their caves.
Someone is deciding to disturb them.

I retreat into a green library,
explore the garden of your body
thinking it can make me free of mine.
We might touch each other into peace,
a private evolution.

If we build a fire at all entrances to the dawn,
we can kiss the red mouths of graves,
or change books into nipples.

YOU ARE A MEDITERRANEAN

Nerves can't reach
passion that spills on floorboards.
You are a wild insomniac
and want a warlock to come to you
in the night with evil magic
and say stop trying to do what is right.
You are a bat who clings upside down
in a corner of the daylight and flies
in the dark while the rest are asleep.
You want to assassinate memory,
but you need rest from this body
which offers no ecstasy
except through clenched teeth.

No purity to reach,
no virginal dawn to wait for and rape,
you pace in a ferment,
you take your voice in your arms
and rock it to sleep.

BICENTENNIAL ANTI-POEM FOR ITALIAN-AMERICAN WOMEN

> *"You are one of only two or three*
> *Italian-American women poets in*
> *this country," said the professor.*
> *"You are a pioneer. There are fewer*
> *of you than Black women poets."*

On the crowded subway,
riding to the prison to teach
Black and Puerto Rican inmates how to write,
I think of the fable of the shoemaker
who struggles to make shoes for the oppressed
while his own go barefoot over the stones.

I remember Grandma, her olive face
wrinkled with resignation,
content just to survive
after giving birth to twenty children,
without orgasmic pleasures or anesthesia.
Grandpa, immigrant adventurer,
who brought his family
steerage passage to the New World;
his shoemaker shop where he labored
over American factory goods
that made his artisan's craft a useless
anachronism; his Code of Honor
which forced him to starve
accepting not a cent of welfare
from anyone but his sons;
his ironic "Code of Honor"
which condoned jealous rages of wife-beating;
Aunt Lizabetta, Aunt Maria-Dominica,
Aunt Raphaela, Aunt Helena, grown women
huddled like girls in their bedroom in Newark,

talking in whispers, not daring
to smoke their American cigarettes
in front of Pa;
the backyard shrine of the virgin,
somber blue-robed woman,
devoid of sexual passions,
to whom Aunt Lizabetta prayed
daily before dying in childbirth,
trying to have *a son*
against doctor's orders
though she had five healthy daughters;
Dr. Guiseppi Ferrara,
purple-heart veteran of World War II,
told he couldn't have a residency
in a big New York Hospital
because of his Italian name;
the mafia jokes, the epithets:
Wop, guinea, dago, grease-ball;
and the stories told by Papa
of Dante, Galileo, Da Vinci,
Marconi, Ferme and Caruso
that stung me with pride
for Italian *men;*
how I was discouraged from school,
told a woman meant for cooking
and bearing doesn't need education.

I remember
Grandma
got out of bed
in the middle of the night
to fetch her *husband* a glass of water
the day she died,
her body wearied
from giving and giving and giving
food and birth.

MY VENUS FLY TRAP IS DYING

because it frightens me.
I've tried to remember to water it.
I keep saying I'll buy it a new pot,
furnish it with fresh earth.
After all, it is a plant and I do love
greenery. But it's carnivorous,
ingesting raw meat, living
insects, engulfing them in heart-
shaped leaves. Other plants wait
for death to give flesh to roots.
I resolve to become a vegetarian.
I've loved and envied plants
for their peacefulness,
their quiet conversion of the sun,
that first all contingent link
between solar energy and animal.
But this Venus Fly Trap
is too much for me.
It will have to die
tossed into the waste can
with the bright red lipstick,
the blood red nail polish.
I no longer wear.
This Venus Fly Trap doesn't
photosynthesize peacefully.
It's trying to become an animal
and I
trying so hard to be a tree
can't bear it.

PARADISE IS NOT A PLACE

*The poets of the future will come when
the infinite servitude of woman will be
broken, when she will live for herself and
by herself . . . she will also be poet! Woman
will find the unknown. "The Great Androgyne
will be created . . . Humanity will be woman and
man, love and thought, tenderness and
strength, grace and energy."*
—Arthur Rimbaud *The Voyant Letters*

Bread in our mouths,
lightning in the belly of a whale,
oceans to slice through with steel fins,
rocks to plant as roses . . .
We drift together on a mattress
into the sea of early sunshine.
Our mattress, Love, floats off to
a deserted tropical island, glides
past battleships, over submarines,
through the tentacles of giant squid.
Tourists turn to look at us
floating on our mattress —
you pressed between my legs over
your shoulders, my hair in your mouth, your
fingers in my ears. They are amazed at our
sailing by on our saffron mattress of mulberry
leaves. We undulate up to the Statue of Liberty.
The old girl winks at us
and lifts her skirt to reveal her hefty pubes.
We float past the wedding cakes of presidents'
     daughters
as we cruise the Potomac shocking Washington ladies.
Our bodies melt into one huge rock.
We are a Magritte Mountain floating out to sea,
victorious in our battle of the sexes.

One day, sailors point and say, "There's
Great Mount Androgyne,
once a fornicating woman and man!"
Missionaries plant a neon cross on top,
enshrining the place where penis merged with clitoris,
and we are at peace in the clouds
with gulls flapping gently around our peak.

LADY GODIVA'S HORSE

She rides me tamely through the town,
seated daintily, naked legs
side-saddling me, a proper lady.
Silk hair covers her shoulders.
Townspeople bow in reverance as we pass
challenging her husband's greedy taxes,
saving Coventry with her nakedness.

Triumphant, we reach
the gates of the city
and she
swings one leg over me,
grips my bare back with her soft thighs.
Her bootless heels
kick my sides
and I run,
her hands loosening my reins,
her body bending close,
her warm weight upon me,
her breasts galloping with my hooves.

And we are one,
beast and lady fused,
one body. She pressed wet to me,
my mane, her hair,
our tail flowing out behind,
the force of her moon-blood
coursing through us, fierce
umbilicus of the moon
pulling us toward the sea.

PEACE PROSPECT

Too many people scribbling on each others' tongues
gagging the cities.
Politics muddle the nature of bodies.
Sexual energy, a force confused, wasted.

While sleep plays out the pain in me,
I have a pleasant dream,
a land inhabited by bright animals
who refuse fire
and eat nothing but leaves.
I count the people I have tried to touch;
my hands melt sand into glass.
We can't manufacture food like vegetation
standing in the light. Photosynthesis
is the trees making love with the sun.
A vague intuition blossoms in my stomach,
a chance for a finer love.
We are a mind-ridden race, incompatible with earth.

A better race will come. I feel
bright animals waiting
for the right genetic moment.

Daniela Gioseffi is a poet and novelist whose work has appeared in such journals as *Ms., Choice, Antaeus, The Nation* and *The Paris Review,* as well as in such noted anthologies as *Contemporaries* (Viking), *Rising Tides* (Simon & Schuster) and *We Become New* (Bantam).

Ms. Gioseffi is also known for her work as a multi-media artist. Her performance of *The Birth Dance of Earth* — the so-called "belly dance" — which includes music and poetry of her own composition, has been critically acclaimed in America and Europe. And she has received award grants in both poetry and multi-media from the Creative Artists Public Service Program of the New York State Council on the Arts.

"I am a neo-pagan reviving the shaminist tradition," Daniela Gioseffi has written about herself. "What I really aspire to is healing some of the rifts in the 20th Century American psyche. In the beginning, poetry, dance, music were all part of the same ritualistic aspiration."

To that end Ms. Gioseffi has spent much of the past several years as a professional actress/singer, as well as a teacher of creative writing — singing, reciting, dancing and performing poetry in colleges, universities, theatres, museums, senior citizen centers, public schools, parks and prisons.

Eggs in The Lake has been issued in a first edition of twelve hundred copies. Seven hundred copies are in paper and four hundred and fifty copies are in cloth. Fifty additional copies have been specially bound by Gene Eckert in quarter cloth and French papers over boards; twenty-six copies are lettered A-Z and signed by Daniela Gioseffi and John Logan; ten copies are numbered I-X, signed by both poets, and include a poem in holograph by Daniela Gioseffi; fourteen copies are numbered i-xiv, signed by both poets, and retained for presentation purposes.